The New Novello Choral Edition

ANTONÍN DVOŘÁK

Mass in D major
Mše D dur
Op.86

for soprano, alto, tenor and bass soloists, SATB and organ
or
SATB (with optional soloists) and orchestra

Edited by Michael Pilkington

Order No: NOV 072491

NOVELLO PUBLISHING LIMITED

It is requested that on all concert notices and programmes acknowledgement is made to 'The New Novello Choral Edition'.

Es wird gebeten, auf sämtlichen Konzertankündigungen und Programmen 'The New Novello Choral Edition' als Quelle zu erwähnen.

Il est exigé que toutes notices et programmes de concerts, comportent des remerciements à 'The New Novello Choral Edition'.

Orchestral material is available on hire from the Publisher.

Orchestermaterial ist beim Verlag erhältlich.

Les partitions d'orchestre sont en location disponibles chez l'editeur.

Permission to reproduce from the Preface of this Edition must be obtained from the Publisher.

Die Erlaubnis, das Vorwort dieser Ausgabe oder Teile desselben zu reproduzieren, muß beim Verlag eingeholt werden.

Le droit de reproduction de ce document à partir de la préface doit être obtenu de l'éditeur.

Cover illustration: first page of the autograph score of the orchestral version of Dvořák's *Mass in D* (courtesy of the British Library).

PREFACE

The Mass in D was composed at the request of Josef Hlávka, architect, patron and founder of the Czech Academy of Sciences and Art, for the consecration of a new chapel beside his castle in Luzany on 11 September 1887. The work was scored for SATB soloists, choir and organ and was completed on 17 June 1887[1]. For a concert performance on 15 April 1888, the organ accompaniment was arranged for two harmoniums, cello and two double basses[2]. Dvořák's regular publisher, N. Simrock, was reluctant to accept the Mass in D for publication, but Novello agreed to publish it on condition that Dvořák provided an orchestral accompaniment. This he did, completing it on 15 June 1892[3]. Novello printed a vocal score, in 1893, with an accompaniment arranged from the orchestral version by Berthold Tours, and a set of parts, but only had the full score hand copied. It is the vocal score of this 1893 edition that this new revised edition supercedes.

An edition of the original organ version was published in 1963 by Robert Carl, adapted for church use by Alois Marie Müller. In 1970 Supraphon published a full score of the orchestral version edited by Jarmil Burghauser. This was based on the autograph of the full score and the Novello vocal score. In 1978 Carus-Verlag published the organ version, edited by Günter Graulich and Paul Horn, based solely on the autograph held in the National Museum in Prague. In 1988 Supraphon published the organ version edited by Burghauser, based on the Prague autograph but also making use of the full score and Novello's published vocal score. Burghauser's use of the Novello vocal score was based on the dubious assumption that '(it) was done in collaboration with the composer'. However, Dvořák was not in England between the end of October 1891 and March 1896, spending October 1892 until the spring of 1894 in America, which would suggest that 'collaboration', if any, was not close. There are a number of changes of text in the Novello vocal score as compared with the Novello full score and all MS sources, apparently in order to bring the words into conformity with the Ordinary of the Roman Catholic Mass. It is by no means certain that the composer approved these alterations. In 1996 Peters Edition issued a vocal score edited by Klaus Burmeister. This provides two keyboard parts: the organ version (on three staves throughout, though in the autograph only, the Kyrie is on three staves) and a new piano reduction made by the editor. There is no information on the sources used, and the vocal dynamics are those of the orchestral version.

When preparing the orchestral version, Dvořák revised his chorus dynamic markings considerably, though making few other changes. This new vocal score is designed to be used for performance with either the 1887 organ version or the 1892 orchestral version, showing both sets of dynamics, and any other differences between the two versions.

As a basis for the organ version the editor has used the copyist's score in the British Library. It is clear that this source contains a number of revisions later taken over into the orchestral version. There are frequent pencil alterations, most of which are clearly corrections of misprints by the copyist; these are accepted here, though noted in the commentary wherever there may be doubt. There are also markings in blue pencil, most of which indicate changes which appear in the autograph full score, implying that they were approved by the composer; indeed, the British Library Catalogue lists this item as 'annotated by the composer'. These markings have also been accepted. This source has not been used or even mentioned in any previous edition.

For the orchestral version, the editor has used the composer's autograph full score, with discrepancies in the Novello copyist's full score and the printed vocal score duly noted. This autograph also has markings. One set (in blue) is clearly by a Novello editor or a conductor, the other (in red) seems to be the composer clarifying queries from the publisher. In most cases the marks have been accepted without comment.

There is one oddity in the orchestration: after bar 73 of the Gloria the third horn is not used, and in fact the remaining movements only specify two horns. In one copy of the Novello full score, someone pencilled in a large independent part for the third horn, but there would seem to be more justification for omitting the instrument altogether.

Michael Pilkington
Old Coulsdon, September 1999

---

1   The autograph is in the National Museum in Prague (Cat. No.VII B 338). A fair copy was made by a copyist, completed on 7 August 1887 (British Library, Loan 69.2)

2   See Jarmil Burghauser, preface to the Supraphon Edition (Prague, 1970). Burghauser also states that Dvořák gave his approval for this arrangement and that it is no longer extant. Interestingly, the fair copy in the British Library has an extra stave added at a later date in a different hand (which could be that of the composer) labelled 'Violoncello and Bass'. This extra stave often clarifies the use of the organ pedals.

3   The score is held in the British Library Loan 69.3

EDITORIAL PROCEDURE

VOICE PARTS
Full size notation shows material found in the organ version and the orchestral version
Full size notation in square brackets shows material found in the organ version only
Small size notation and slurs and hairpins with 'cuts' show material found in the orchestral version only
Small size notation and slurs and hairpins with 'cuts' in square brackets show editorial additions

ORGAN
Brackets and strokes show the work of the editor; small notes are occasionally used where the orchestral version is scored for organ only, and can be ignored in performance with organ.

SOURCES

A	British Library Loan 69.2
	A fair copy of the composer's autograph of the organ version (held in the National Museum (Prague), VII B 338), dated 7 August 1887, and containing revisions by the composer.
Ai	British Library Loan 69.2
	An extra stave added at a later date (possibly by the composer?) labelled 'Violoncello & Bass'.
B	British Library Loan 69.3
	Composer's autograph of the full score, dated 15 June 1892
C	Supraphon edition (1970-1988) edited by Jarmil Burghauser.
Ci	Supraphon Full Score (1970)
Cii	Supraphon Vocal Score (1988)
D	Novello edition (1893)
Di	Novello Full Score (1893)
Dii	Novello Vocal Score (1893)
E	Carus-Verlag Vocal Score (1978), edited by Günter Graulich and Paul Horn
F	Peters Vocal Score (1996), edited by Klaus Burmeister (agrees with **Cii** unless otherwise stated).

COMMENTARY

Kyrie
Two bars of introduction were added when Dvořák made the orchestral version. Even then it appears to have been an afterthought, as they have been pasted in over the names of the strings.
Bar

14	Organ L.H.: bass dotted minims added to **A** in pencil and included in **Ai**; not in **Cii** or **E**.
43	Organ L.H.: last bass note marked 'Ped.' In pencil in **A** and given in **Ai** and **F**; not in **Cii** or **E**. Confirmed by double basses in **B**.
59	See notes below on use of chorus, small chorus and solo voices.
61	Dvořák appears to use 'sotto voce' and 'm.v.' (mezza voce) interchangeably; previous editors have used 'sotto voce' in all cases. Here the terms are given as used by the composer, so that performers can decide for themselves whether any difference is intended.
72	Organ L.H.: last two notes marked 'Ped.' in **A** in pencil, and given in **Ai**; not in **Cii** or **E**. In this case not confirmed by double basses in **B**.
73-74	See notes below on use of chorus, small chorus and solo voices.

Gloria

10	Alto note 3: f♯' in **A** and **B** clearly in error.
23-4	*cresc.* and hairpins added to **B** in blue; not in **D**, given in **Ci** without comment, but a sensible editorial addition.
30	Organ R.H. beat 3: **Cii** and **E** have d♯' and f♯', not f♯' and a♯'; oddly **A** has a ♯ to the f♯', but there is no d' in **B** or **D**.

36	Alternative text in **B** (followed by **F**), which originally had the same rhythm as **A**, but the first quaver was deleted before the words were added.
73	In **A** original 'Poco meno mosso' altered in pencil to 'Moderato'; in **B** 'Moderato' is altered to 'Andante', with 'con moto' and the metronome mark added later.
73-118	**B** scored for organ only; small size notation and slurs, ties and hairpins with 'cuts' are taken from **B**.
74	See notes below on use of chorus, small chorus and solo voices.
88, 90	Tempo marks added in blue, **A**. Present in **B**, but without 'poco'.
94-7	Dvořák omits 'Deus'; main text as in **A**, **B**, **Di**, **E**; italic text from **Dii** followed by **C**.
99-113	See notes below on use of chorus, small chorus and solo voices.
118	Bass last note: **A** has *f* for *p*.
118-133	See notes below on use of chorus, small chorus and solo voices.
119	**A** has 'Un poco lento' altered in pencil to 'Andante'; **B** has 'Andante' altered to 'Meno mosso'.
123	Alto: **B** had an extra quaver a' between beats 2 and 3; this was deleted, but in such a way that the upper part of the deleting stroke could be read as a b'. **C** and **D** read it thus, and alter the rhythm of the whole bar into 6 quavers (including the extra b') and a crotchet. The following bar makes the correct reading obvious.
146	Tenor: **A** has b, b, with the second b corrected by the copyist to c♯'. In **B** the first note could be b or c', but the second is clearly c♯'. **C** and **D** give two c♯s, **E** gives two bs, neither **C** nor **E** makes any comment on this bar.
182	The composer altered the actual notes when making the orchestral version, to give the basses a scale as in bar 180 rather than imitating organ R.H. in bar 181 with L.H. in bar 182.
190-2	Bass: **A** and **B** give B, A; **Cii** agrees, but follows **D** in altering orchestral version to G, d (though referring this reading to **B** in error); **E** gives B, d, **F** gives G, d without comment. The cadence B, A, is possible with the basses descending phrase in bar 189, but loses its point with the revised bass part in that bar in the orchestral version. In spite of the trombones, this cadence for the chorus seems improbable, perhaps copying the alto notes in error; the reading offered here avoids doubling the major third, creating octaves with the tenor, leaping from bar 189 (in organ version) or ending with a second inversion chord.

Credo

1	**A** has 'Allegro non troppo' altered to 'Allegro moderato'. See notes below on use of chorus, small chorus and solo voices.
5	Also bars 24, 328, 336, 386, 412: Alternative text from **Dii**, followed by **C** but not **E**. Since the main text appears in all MSS, that is, through several revisions, it seems likely that these modifications to the Mass text were intended by Dvořák.
59-86	In the orchestra full chords are held by wind and brass, while all strings play chords in the rhythm shown above the stave.
119	See notes below on use of chorus, small chorus and solo voices.
140	Organ R.H. note 3: **Di** has a flat added to the a, clearly added by another hand, but followed by **Dii**. There is no authority for this flat, given in none of the sources, or any modern editions.
161	In **B** from here to bar 182 there is only one stave for strings, marked 'C.B.', **Di** has copied this into the cello stave, followed by **Ci**, without comment, but adding 'senza sord'. Double bass alone is probably correct.
177-8	Alto underlay: **A** slurs as tenors and basses, but the underlay for these and previous bars is shown by ✕ signs as following the sopranos; **B** slurs in bar 178, followed by **C** and **D**. **E** slurs as tenors and basses.
183	Dynamics added to **A** in blue here and for organ in bar 187.
183-6	**A**: tenor and bass notes altered in blue, and carried over to **B**.
191-4	**A**: soprano, tenor and bass notes altered in red ink, and carried over to **B**.
207-10	**A**: tenor and bass altered in ink, and carried over to **B**. None of these changes is accepted as applying to the organ version by **Cii** or **E**. The original notes in **A** are here given small.
242	'Più allegro' in **A** altered in pencil to 'Tempo I'; 'Tempo I' and 'meno' added in red to **B**, with the metronome mark added in blue.
260-7	**B** has no accompaniment in these bars, followed by **D**; **Ci** notes the example of bars 221-249 and adds parts for oboes and bassoons that follow the organ score, but adjusting to fit tenor in bar 261. Given without comment in **F**, and accepted in this edition.

312-3	Organ R.H.: alto originally read f′ minim, e′♮ crotchet, f′ crotchet; L.H. tenor read b a g c′, all crotchets; the bass retained the upper f tied from the previous bar; all given thus in **Cii**, **E** and **F**. Text in **A** clearly altered and confirmed by **B**.
358	Organ L.H. note 3: f, scratched out in **A** but no rest added; given in **Cii** and **E**; no f in **B** or **D**.
407	Tenor note 3: c′ in **B**, **Ci**, **D** and **F**; comparison with soprano bar 415 suggests this is an error.
428-448	Organ L.H. (also bb.436-7, 444-5); the crotchets are a revision in **A**, not present in **Cii** or **E**.

Sanctus

| 98-99 | Small print crotchet chords, no held D in bass, and no 'attacca' in **B**, **Ci** and **Di**. |

Benedictus

1-20	Originally arranged for strings in **B** but then crossed out and the organ version retained with a few minor changes; small notes and slurs and ties with 'cuts' are editorial markings and come from this source.
24	Soprano note 2: given as f′ in all MSS, **Di** has this corrected to g′, agreed by all editors.
36	The alteration of tenor note 3 from b♭ to a♭ in **B** meant a change of rhythm in the accompanying instruments, though Dvořák only noticed this after he had written the old dotted minim crotchet rhythm and had to make a correction. Though **E** gives the organ version rhythm for the organ accompaniment it strangely gives the tenors the a♭. **F** shows both versions of tenor part, but only the organ version of the accompaniment.
61-76	Organ only in **B**, small notes and slurs and ties with 'cuts' are editorial markings and come from this source.

Agnus Dei

10	Alto last quaver: d′ in **A**, **Cii** and **E**, altered to a clear c♯′ in **B**, followed by **D** (though this seems to have started life as a d) and **Ci**. The accompanying flute melody ends the bar with a quaver b′, which could possibly be read as a c♯″; **D** and **F** have b′, **Ci** has c♯″. Comparison with the entries for soprano, tenor and bass suggest strongly that the alto c′ is the error, and that it should remain d′, with the flute on b′.
20	**E** ends pedal after first quaver, **Cii** ends after bar 21; both start pedal again with minim on beat 3 at bar 24. **A** has no pedal indications in this section and in **Ai** double bass plays throughout.
55	Tenor: **A** and **E** have a dotted minim d; **Cii** has a crotchet d, but notes original reading as being indistinct. **B** does not help, being after a page turn and showing an empty bar! **Di** offers both crotchet f♯ and crotchet d (!) and **Dii** and **F** choose the crotchet f♯.
55-56	**A** has soprano divisi in 3 and given thus in **B**, **C**, **D** and **E**. However, in **A** the lowest part has been copied into the alto as shown here in small print, and the lowest part deleted from the soprano line, all in pencil. In **B** the lower two parts have been copied into the alto, in pencil, but the soprano parts have not been deleted; this seems to be a recommendation of the Novello editor, and was not accepted in **D**.
	Organ: **Ci** and **E** have editorial 'Ped.' in this bar and **F** an octave D on the pedal stave, but in **A** the double bass does not start playing until bar 57, where 'Ped.' is also given. In **B**, **Ci** and **Di** the double basses only start in bar 59.

CHORUS, SMALL CHORUS AND SOLO VOICES

The instructions given in the sources are rather confused, and it appears that Dvořák changed his mind several times. The following remarks cover the main points.

Organ version
Kyrie

| 59 | **A** 'Solo' for all voices, until 'Tutti' (added in blue) in bars 73 and 74; however, **A** has deleted 'Solo' in pencil for soprano, tenor and bass, though not Alto, nor are the 'Tuttis' deleted. This suggests the passage could be sung by the chorus if desired. **Cii** and **E** give both 'Solo' and 'Tutti' without comment. |

Gloria

74   **A** has 'Soli' for soprano and 'Solo' (sic) for alto added in blue, and at bar 82 both tenor and bass are marked 'Solo' (sic) in blue. Bars 90 and 92 have 'Tutti' also in blue. Neither **Cii**, **E** nor **F** give any of these markings, leaving the passage as full chorus. Perhaps the section could be sung with four voices to a part, as in the orchestral version.

99   **A** has 'Solo' for soprano, deleted in blue. **Cii** and **E** have 'Solo' here, and in bars 101 (tenor), 107 (alto) and 109 (bass), and all editors return to 'Tutti' at bar 113. None of these appear in **A**.

118   It seems likely in this passage that Dvořák originally intended some parts to be solo and some chorus, but changed his mind and decided the whole passage should remain full chorus. Bass, beat 4: **Cii** and **E** have 'Solo', but nothing is marked in **A**. Bar 121, tenor, bar 126, soprano: **A** has 'Solo' deleted in blue; **Cii** and **E** have 'Solo'. At bar 127 the 'Tutti' for tenor and bass is not deleted in **A** and is given in **Cii** but not **F**; at bar 129 'Solo' for alto is deleted and 'Tutti' added, all in blue, but **Cii** and **E** have 'Solo'. Bar 133: 'Tutti' for soprano and alto deleted in blue **A**, given in **Cii** and **E**, but not **F**.

Credo

Though Alto at bar 119 and Bass at bar 133 are marked 'Solo' in **A**, the soprano at 146 and tenor at 161 have no marking. Since all four voices are marked 'Tutti' at 183 (in blue) this is probably an oversight. **Cii** and **E** mark bar 146 'Solo', but have 'Tutti' for all voices at bars 160-1. These markings are taken from the orchestral version, see below.

Orchestral version

B has a note at the bottom of the title page: 'Remark! Small Chorus means to be sung <u>by 4 voices on each part</u>. Solo would also be all right.'

Kyrie

59   **B** has note: 'Small chorus of 4 voices or solo if preferred.'

73-74   **B** has 'Tutti' for all voices, agreed by **Ci**; **Di** had these crossed out for all voices, for some reason, though there is no later 'Tutti' and **Dii** gives 'Tutti' here.

Gloria

74   **B** has a footnote 'Small Chorus of 4 voices only or <u>Solo if pleased</u>, and so on the whole Mass.'

101   Tenor, also bar 103 soprano: **B** has 'or Solo' added in red, but the alto and bass entries are merely marked 'Alti' and 'Bassi'. The 'Tutti' markings in bar 121 (Tenor) and 126 (Soprano) seem merely cautionary, since all voices returned to 'Tutti' at bar 113.

Credo

B has footnote: '4 Alti only throughout the whole piece, and not Solo!' (not by Dvořák, according to **Ci** notes). On the other hand, at bar 119 **B** has 'Small Chorus or Solo' added in red. In **B** 'Tutti' is marked at bars 160-1, rather than at 183, as given in **A**. Given at bb.160-1 in **Cii** and **E**.

★ ★ ★ ★

This new edition of the *Mass in D* follows the layout of the previous edition (catalogue number NOV 070087) page for page, to allow this new edition to be used side-by-side with the edition it supersedes.

MASS IN D MAJOR
KYRIE

* see Preface

2

* see Preface

4

* see Preface   † bass: all notes in this bar staccato in **B**   senza Ped.

5

* soprano note 2: e in **B**   † see Preface

6

* A has c" ♪ ·, b' o ·

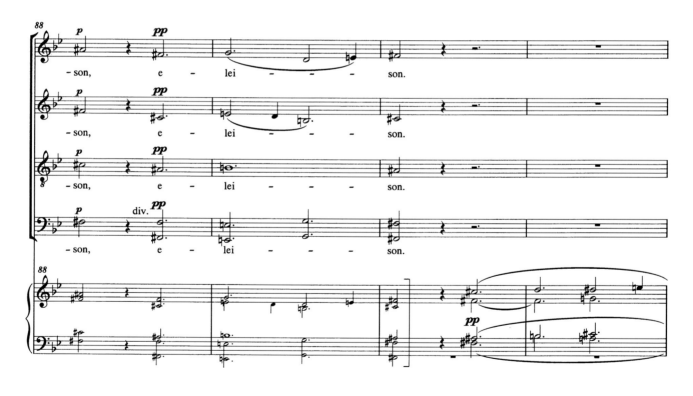

* for rehearsal only

GLORIA

12

* see Preface   ** tenor: ♩ ♩ ♫, **B**   † ♩ ♫, all voices **B**

13

* for rehearsal only   ** see Preface

14

* bass note 1: ♪ 7 in **B**   † bass: staccato in **B** only, omitted in **D**

* staccato dots only given for soprano, A

* see Preface

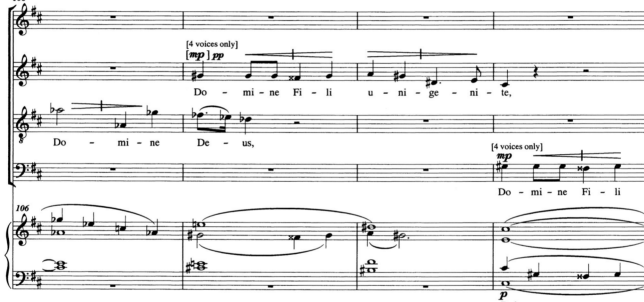

* tenor and bass: staccato marking **B**

* small note from **B**   ** for rehearsal only   † alto note 2 has ♯ in **B**   †† see Preface

24

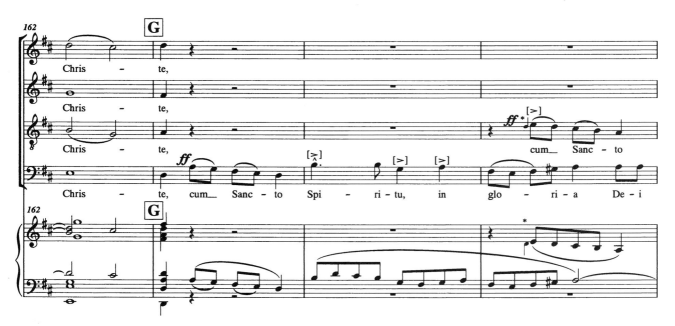

* tenor and RH, note 1: ♩ d in **B**

* tenor and bass: ♩♩♩ ♪ in A   † soprano notes 2-4: staccato from B

* in **B**   ** bass note 5: f♮ in **B**   † bass: ![notation] in all MS sources; ![notation] in **D**, see Preface

CREDO

29

* see Preface

* alto: crotchet in **B**

* lower bass note in **B**   † see Preface

* tenor note 3: c in **B, C**

* see Preface

* see Preface

* see Preface

* see Preface

* see Preface

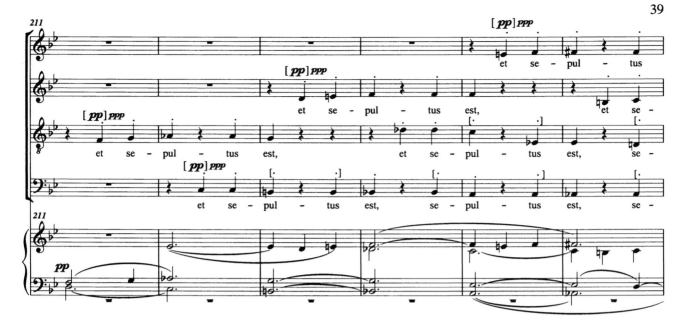

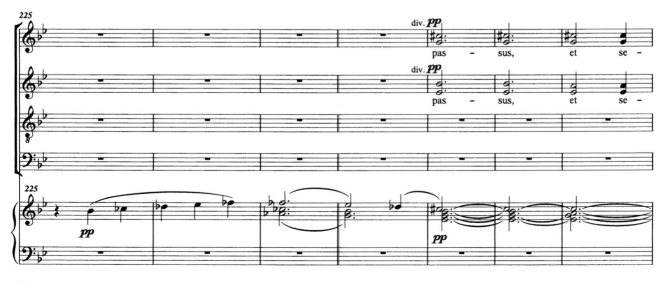

* for rehearsal only

40

* see Preface

* see Preface   † tenor notes1 and 2: e♭, d in **B**

* organ LH: a missing in A, supplied from B

44

* see Preface

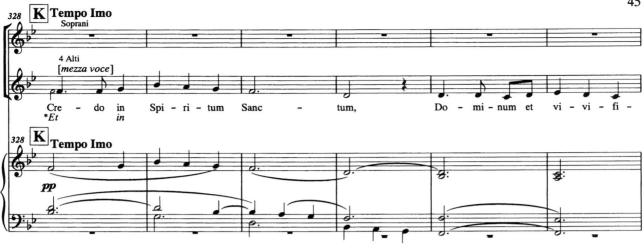

* see Preface † 𝅗𝅥. in **B** and **Dii**

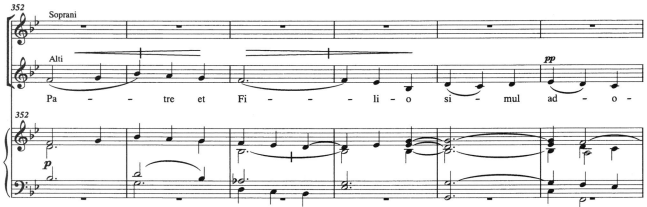

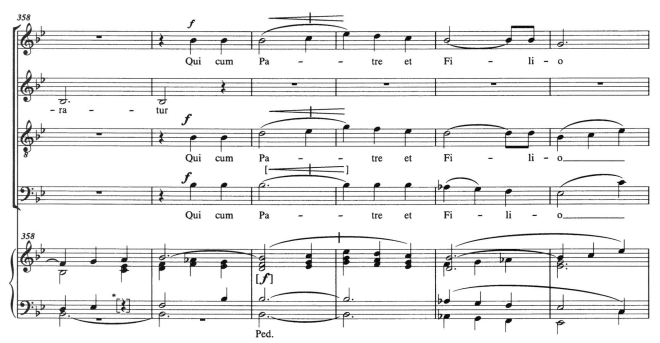

* see Preface

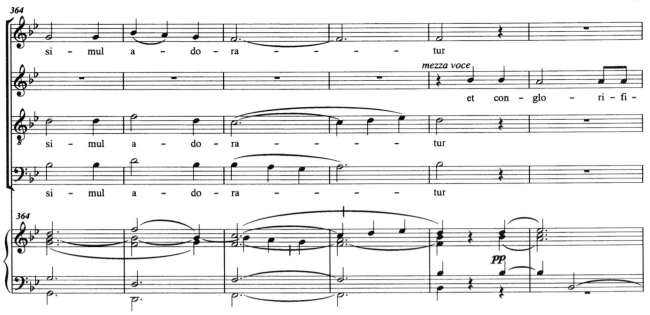

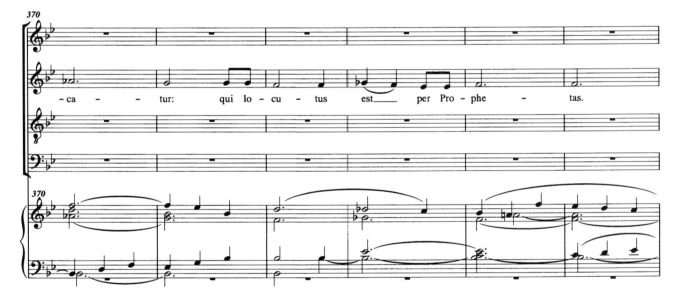

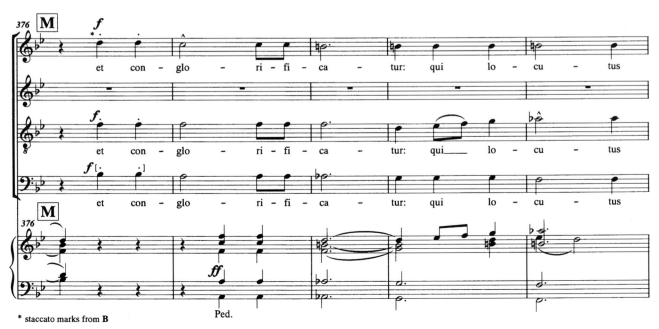

* staccato marks from **B**

48

* see Preface   Ped.

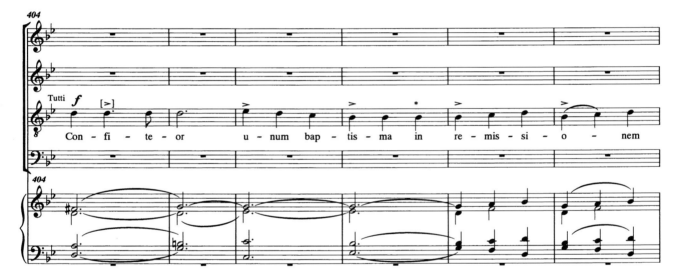

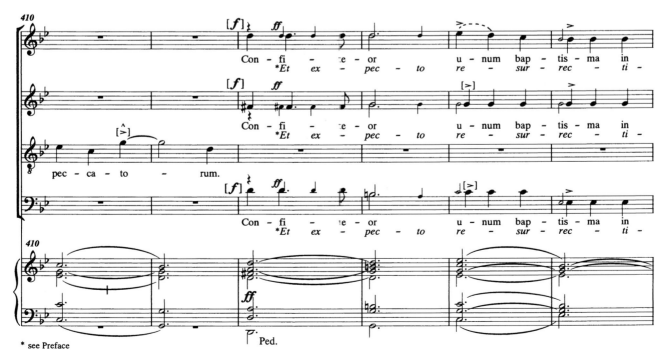

* see Preface

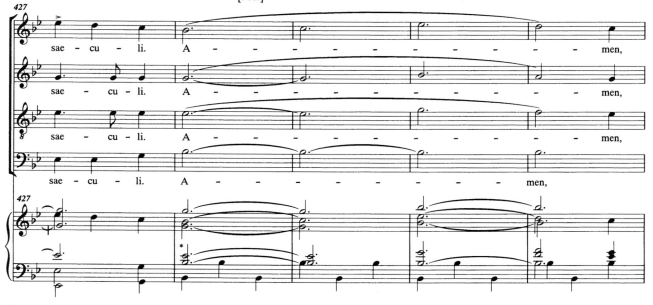

* see Preface

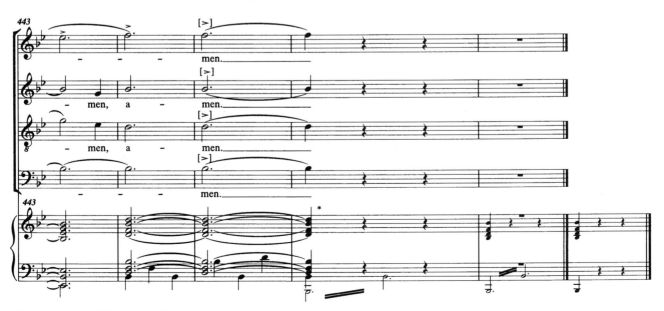

* small notes show additional music in **B**

SANCTUS

* alto note 2: f ' in **A**, editors give g ', as in **B**

* alternative words from **B**   † see Preface

BENEDICTUS

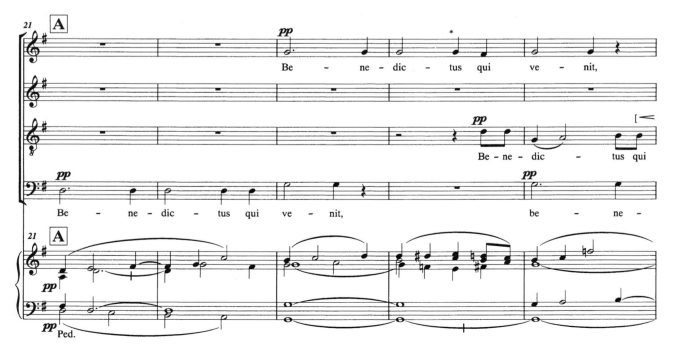

Be - ne - dic - tus qui ve - nit,

Be - ne - dic - tus qui

Be - ne - dic - tus qui ve - nit, be - ne

* see Preface

* see Preface

* alto note 1: g in **A**   † tenor: ♪ ⅞ ⁊ ‡ in **B**

* lower bass note from **B**

* lower bass note 3: lower note from **B**

AGNUS DEI

* see Preface

68

* soprano note 3: b' in **A,B,D**, but see organ, and bar 28.

senza Ped.

70

† see Preface   * RH note 2: natural in all sources, but should perhaps be sharp

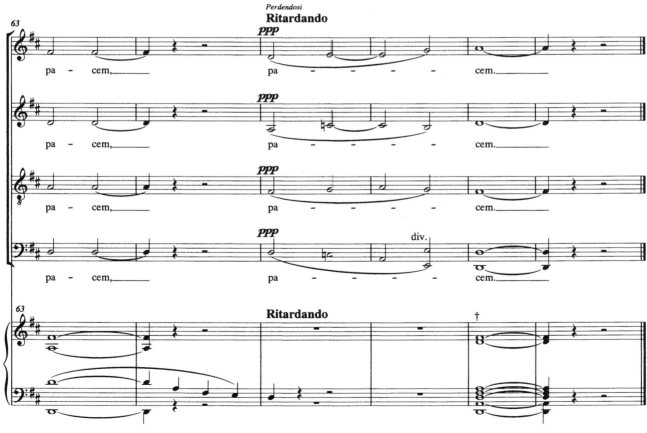

* alternative underlay from **B**   ** organ LH: both ds semibreves in **A**, in error.   † organ RH: f ' added in pencil in **A**, present in **B**

Published by Novello Publishing Limited
Printed and bound in Great Britain by Caligraving Limited